KUMON WRITING WORKBOOKS

Writing

Table of Contents

Level ☆

Date / /

Name

Score /100

1 Insert commas to separate the items in each series.

5 points each

(1) They bought lettuce__ tomatoes__ cucumbers__ and onions for the salad.

(2) I packed my swimsuit__ sandals__ towel__ and snorkel for our trip.

(3) Do you want carrots__ an apple__ or yogurt for your snack today?

(4) She has not traveled to Africa__ Europe__ or Australia.

Hint: Commas separate items in a list of three or more items, called a series. When a conjunction such as *and* or *or* joins the last two items in a series, a comma is used before the conjunction.

(5) Dollars__ quarters__ nickels__ and pennies were in my pocket.

2 Combine the sentences by writing the items in a series. Use commas and the conjunction in the brackets.

5 points each

(1) I like eggplant. I like mushrooms. I like green beans.   [and]

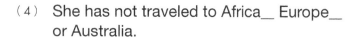

I like eggplant, mushrooms, and green beans.

(2) The first aid kit has bandages. The first aid kit has alcohol wipes. The first aid kit has adhesive tape.   [and]

_____

(3) My brother doesn't play the piano. My brother doesn't play the guitar. My brother doesn't play the violin.   [or]

_____

(4) People are mammals. Chimpanzees are mammals. Dolphins are mammals.   [and]

_____

(5) He doesn't have a French stamp. He doesn't have a Japanese stamp. He doesn't have a Peruvian stamp.   [or]

_____

3 Combine each sentence pair with a comma and the conjunction in the brackets.

5 points each

(1) Our room is finished. The paint must dry.   [but]

Our room is finished, but the paint must dry.

(2) The students walked to school. They played during recess.   [and]

_____

(3) We had fun at the park. We asked if we could go again.   [so]

_____

(4) The snow fell quickly. It melted when it hit the ground.   [yet]

_____

_____

Hint: A comma and a conjunction can join two simple sentences together.

(5) The couple wanted to play tennis. The court was wet.   [but]

_____

_____

4 Combine each sentence pair with a comma and a conjunction from the box.   5 points each

| and | or | so | yet | but |

(1) We wanted to see a movie. There weren't any good ones playing.

We wanted to see a movie but there weren't any good ones playing.

(2) The bald eagle is rare. It is the symbol of the United States.

The bald eagle is rare _____.

(3) They could go together in a car. They could ride their bicycles.

They could go together in a car _____.

(4) Ants are tiny. They are strong for their size.

Ants are tiny _____.

(5) We closed the lid on the garbage can tightly. Raccoons won't get inside it.

We closed the lid on the garbage can tightly _____

_____.

You're off to a great start!

Punctuation
Review

2

Date / /

Name

Level ⭐

Score / 100

1 Complete each sentence with punctuation marks around the quotations.

5 points each

(1) The principal said__ __Welcome to school__ __

(2) __Everyone is aboard__ __ the captain announced.

(3) __What number is in the hundredths place__ __ our teacher asked.

(4) __I disliked that movie__ __ my friend said.

(5) The librarian asked__ __What is the name of the author__ __

> **Hint:** Quotation marks show the beginning and end of a quotation. Pay close attention to the locations of other punctuation, like commas and periods, when using quotation marks.

2 Complete each sentence with punctuation.

5 points each

(1) Sarah said__ "I love to hike in the fall__"

(2) "We painted a mural during art class__" the boy said.

(3) "Can you reach the top shelf___" her little sister asked.

(4) Donald said__ "My teacher's name is Mr. Klingborg__"

(5) My neighbor asked__ "Do you want to play soccer___"

3 Rewrite each sentence with punctuation and capitalization.

5 points each

(1) the art teacher said clean your brushes

_____

(2) i told allan meet me when you finish your chores

_____

(3) our coach yelled defense

_____

(4) the woman asked may i please have a napkin

_____

(5) the announcer said the score is two to one

_____

(6) a flight attendant told us please buckle your seat belts

_____

(7) our conductor exclaimed that was wonderful

_____

_____

(8) the mail carrier said this is not enough postage

_____

(9) may I go to angelas house tamra asked

_____

(10) my science teacher said blood moves through the blood vessels

_____

Keep it up!

Direct / Indirect Speech

Date / /

Name

Score

/100

1 Complete the direct-speech sentences based on the illustration.

5 points each

"Why do we recycle?"

"We recycle to reuse materials."

Robin

Adam

Evan

"We recycle to create less trash."

"We recycle to protect animals."

(1) The teacher asked _"Why do we recycle?"_

(2) Robin said _____

(3) Adam said _____

(4) Evan said _____

Hint: In direct speech, you repeat the speaker's exact words. In indirect speech, you report what the person has said without using his or her exact words.

2 Complete the indirect-speech sentences based on the illustration. Write *that* in the box, and change the pronoun accordingly.

5 points each

"My project is about irrigation."

"I would like to see it in action."

"You should be very proud."

"Mr. Stevens helped me a lot."

Isabel

Jill

Jack

Bern

(1) Isabel said | that | _her project is about irrigation_ .

(2) Jill said | _____ | _____ .

(3) Jack said | _____ | _____ .

(4) Principal Bern said | _____ | _____ .

3 Write *D* next to each sentence that includes direct speech. Write *I* next to each sentence that includes indirect speech.

6 points each

(1) Jack exclaimed, "I got a new bicycle for my birthday!" ———

(2) My elderly grandmother said that she needs new glasses. ———

(3) The president said that he will veto the bill. ———

(4) The stranger asked, "Do you have the time?" ———

(5) Her teacher asked if she was ready to give her speech. ———

4 Correct the punctuation in each sentence.

6 points each

(1) The queen said I love this book!

_____

(2) Our cousins told us "that Thanksgiving dinner would be at their house."

_____

(3) My father asked Did you finish your chores

_____

(4) I heard someone ask if "the store would be closing soon."

_____

(5) The radio announcer said Snow is likely all day tomorrow

_____

Well done.

_____

Complex Sentences

Review

Level ★

Date   /   /   Name

Score   /100

1 Combine each sentence pair with the conjunction in the brackets.   5 points each

(1) We used to ski down that mountain. It got too warm.   [before]

We used to ski down that mountain _before it got too warm_ .

(2) My sister chopped the onions. I stirred the soup.   [while]

My sister chopped the onions _____ .

(3) You can visit your friends. Your mother agrees.   [if]

You can visit your friends _____ .

(4) The nurse found the crutches. The supplies are stored.   [where]

The nurse found the crutches _____ .

> **Don't forget!**
>
> A **complex sentence** has two or more simple sentences that are connected by a conjunction such as *before, after,* or *while.*

2 Combine the sentences into a complex sentence with a conjunction from the box. You can use each conjunction more than once.   6 points each

before	while	if	where

(1) They went to the school library. The yearbooks are kept.

They went to the school library _____ .

(2) The boy will not be punished. He has a good excuse for being late.

The boy will not be punished _____ .

(3) Make sure the box stays sealed. You transport it.

Make sure the box stays sealed _____ .

(4) The producer cued the camera operator. The reporter began the news.

The producer cued the camera operator _____ .

(5) Her cousin loaded the dirty clothes. She started the washing machine.

Her cousin loaded the dirty clothes _____ .

3 Combine each sentence pair with the conjunction in the brackets.

5 points each

(1) The hippopotamus rolled in the mud. He ate some grass.   [after]

The hippopotamus rolled in the mud

after he ate some grass .

(2) Caitlin's story was believable. Her characters were lifelike.   [because]

Caitlin's story was believable _____ .

(3) I borrowed my brother's bike. My bike had a flat tire.   [when]

I borrowed my brother's bike _____ .

(4) The gymnast performed so well. The judges gave her top scores.   [that]

The gymnast performed so well _____

_____ .

4 Combine the sentences into a complex sentence with a conjunction from the box. You can use each conjunction more than once.

6 points each

after	because	when	that

(1) We are looking for a dictionary. We don't know a word's meaning.

We are looking for a dictionary _____ .

(2) My mother put the pan into the oven. She poured the cake batter into the pan.

My mother put the pan into the oven _____ .

(3) The violinist practiced the song so often. He memorized it.

The violinist practiced the song so often _____ .

(4) The choir sang a song. It was their turn to perform.

The choir sang a song _____ .

(5) Wendy practices her backhand. She wants to improve.

Wendy practices her backhand _____ .

Hooray for you!

Complex Sentences
Review

5

Level ☆

Score
/100

Date   /   /

Name

1 Combine the sentences into a complex sentence with the conjunction *since* and a comma.

5 points each

(1) Our team improved. We are doing better in the tournaments.

Since our team improved, we are doing better in the tournaments.

(2) The planetarium closed. They couldn't see the exhibit anymore.

_____ couldn't see the exhibit anymore.

(3) Peter had swimming lessons. He can swim faster.

_____ can swim faster.

(4) Summer began. More people became dehydrated.

_____ people became dehydrated.

(5) The motorcycle broke down. Its rider has been walking.

_____ rider has been walking.

2 Combine the sentences into a complex sentence with the conjunction *if* and a comma.

5 points each

(1) The company advertises. More people will know about it.

_____ people will know about it.

(2) The jacket is reversible. You can wear it two different ways.

_____ can wear it two different ways.

(3) We take a different route. We won't sit in traffic.

_____ won't sit in traffic.

(4) She wants to learn more. She can read the brochure.

_____ can read the brochure.

(5) We leave our cat home alone. She cries and scratches the furniture.

_____ cries and scratches the furniture.

3 Combine the sentences into a complex sentence with the conjunction *although* and a comma.

5 points each

(1) He doesn't speak English. He will learn quickly.

_____ will learn quickly.

(2) Reptiles and birds are different. They both lay eggs.

_____

both lay eggs.

(3) The painting was not complete. It was already beautiful.

_____ was already beautiful.

(4) The tribes didn't have coins or dollars. They did conduct business.

_____

_____ did conduct business.

4 Combine the sentences into a complex sentence with the conjunction *as* and a comma.

6 points each

(1) I had to meet a friend. I got ready to leave.

_____ got ready to leave.

(2) My brother didn't save his allowance. He couldn't buy the toy.

_____ couldn't buy the toy.

(3) We all play instruments. We decided to start a band.

_____ decided to start a band.

(4) The current was strong. They didn't go into the ocean.

_____ didn't go into the ocean.

(5) Apples are nutritious. We eat them often.

_____ eat them often.

You rock!

Independent and Dependent Clauses

6

Level ☆

Date / /

Name

Score /100

---

1 Complete each sentence with an independent clause from the box.

5 points each

The puppy limped	Tornadoes can occur in spring
The nature reserve is large	You need glasses

(1) _____
because the air temperature changes.

(2) _____
so it will house many animals.

(3) _____
since he hurt his leg.

(4) _____
if you can't see the board.

> **Don't forget!**
>
> A **clause** is a group of words that has a subject and a verb. A complex sentence has an **independent clause** and a **dependent clause**. The independent clause can stand alone as a sentence. The dependent clause cannot.

---

2 Read each incomplete and complete sentence. Write the complete sentence in the space provided.

5 points each

(1) Who tried to shoot from the free-throw line.
The star player shot the ball.   The star player shot the ball

(2) The sea rose substantially.
If the seas rise.   _____

(3) That helps to pay for cheerleading uniforms.
We raised money.   _____

(4) Though the teacher gave extra time.
The teacher said, "Time is up."   _____

3 Complete each sentence with an independent clause from the box.

6 points each

I am grateful	The leaves have changed color
Elephants roam	She brought her blanket
the man wore a heavy suit	

(1) _____
since the weather became colder.

(2) _____ where
they can find food.

(3) Although it was hot out, _____
_____.

(4) _____ whenever my brother
helps me with my homework.

(5) _____ in case they wanted
to picnic.

4 Write the independent clause of each sentence in the space provided.

6 points each

(1) A fossil was found, but it was not well preserved. _____

(2) The bird could fly after its wing healed. _____

(3) I like to ride my bike even when it is raining. _____

(4) Whenever he heard music, Bill loved to sing along. _____

(5) He sold a comic book whenever a fan made him a good offer.

_____

Take a bow!

7

Independent and Dependent Clauses

Level ☆

Date / /

Name

Score

/100

1 Complete each sentence with a dependent clause from the box.

5 points each

until we couldn't anymore.	If there is an emergency,
where he could see all the players.	
before we could catch it.	If it begins to rain,

(1) _____ the nurse has a first aid kit.

(2) We stayed awake _____

(3) Her dog jumped over the fence _____

_____

(4) _____ we will have to postpone the volleyball match.

(5) The scout sat in the bleachers _____

_____

2 Write *IC* next to each independent clause. Write *DC* next to each dependent clause.

5 points each

(1) If we can pay for a new set of paintbrushes. _____DC_____

(2) My sister worked. _____

(3) Since you haven't seen a movie. _____

(4) Although it was from the 1950s. _____

(5) We can watch one together. _____

Hint: A dependent clause does not express a complete thought but does include a subject and a verb.

3 Circle the independent clause and underline the dependent clause of each sentence.

5 points each

(1) Although he has read many types of books, he likes historical fiction the best.

(2) Radio stations broadcast popular songs until people no longer like them.

(3) Before I go to bed, I always brush my teeth.

(4) The inventor believed in his device before anyone else liked it.

(5) After she writes a story, she draws corresponding illustrations.

4 Write the dependent clause of each sentence in the space provided.

5 points each

(1) The scouts planned a wilderness trip where they could hike to an old fort.

where they could hike
to an old fort

(2) We haven't had one warm day since we celebrated Thanksgiving.

_____
_____

(3) Our parents arrived before we could finish our game.

_____
_____

(4) Until Mom wakes up, we should be quiet.

_____

(5) Although he loves strawberry ice cream, he didn't want any.

_____
_____

You're doing great!

8

Independent and Dependent Clauses

Level

Date
/ /

Name

Score

/100

1   Write the independent clause of each sentence in the space provided.   5 points each

(1)   Maya hopes to exhibit her photographs so others will see her work.

   _____

   _____

(2)   When it gets very hot, we go to the pool.

   _____

(3)   Since the summer began, they have been playing outside longer.

   _____

   _____

(4)   Protesters marched because they wanted more money for schools.

   _____

(5)   Even though I asked her to stop, my sister persisted.

   _____

2   Write the dependent clause of each sentence in the space provided.   5 points each

(1)   After I took a nap, I felt rested.

   _____

(2)   We could still smell the cookies baking even though the oven door was closed.

   _____

   _____

(3)   The store advertised the sale so every passing person would see.

   _____

   _____

(4)   Before the show ended, the performers had already received two standing ovations.

   _____

(5)   I diverted their attention while my brother captured the flag.

   _____

3 Use your own words to write an independent clause for each sentence. Use the illustration as a guide, and use a form of the verb in the brackets.

5 points each

(1) Even though she was tired, _____

_____. [wash]

(2) While her friend read a comic book, _____

_____. [read]

(3) If we hurry, _____

_____. [catch]

(4) _____

_____ although our boat was close. [surface]

(5) _____

_____ when the groceries arrived. [carry]

(6) _____

_____ whenever they had time. [ride]

(7) _____

_____ so she can fly to another planet one day.
[want]

(8) _____

_____ although it was heavy. [lift]

(9) _____

_____ until they reached the edge of the forest.
[hop]

(10) _____

_____ after they finished school for the day.
[practice]

You should
be proud.

Noun Clauses

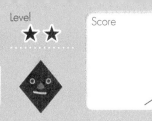

1 Write the dependent clause of each sentence in the space provided.

6 points each

(1) Steven asked the teacher why leaves change color.

_____

(2) My sister was upset that she didn't ace her test.

_____

(3) The magician showed us how he performed the trick.

_____

(4) The marching band followed where the band-leader walked.

_____

(5) The audience member wanted to know how the play would end.

_____

> **Don't forget!**
>
> A **noun clause** is a dependent clause that acts as a noun. Like a noun, a noun clause can be the subject or object of a sentence.
>
> For example: I found <u>the book.</u>   I found <u>what I had been looking for.</u>
>
>   object / noun   noun clause

2 Complete each sentence with a noun clause from the box.

5 points each

that we finished our essays on time	what my friend was thinking
how the coach did the jump	that she could wear her favorite dress

(1) Jeanine was hoping _____.

(2) All the swimmers watched _____.

(3) Our teacher seemed pleased _____.

(4) I wanted to hear _____.

3 Complete the answer to each question with a noun clause from the sentence. 5 points each

(1) The movie critic did not say when the movie takes place.
What did the movie critic not say?

The movie critic did not say _____.

(2) Ben asked why glue is sticky.
What did Ben ask?

Ben asked _____.

(3) The lady asked what I want to be when I grow up.
What did the lady ask?

The lady asked _____.

(4) Our teacher showed us how she got electricity from a potato.
What did our teacher show us?

Our teacher showed us _____.

(5) The lady didn't know where the post office was.
What didn't the lady know?

The lady didn't know _____.

(6) Jennifer wants to know where the kitten went.
What does Jennifer want to know?

Jennifer wants to know _____.

(7) The veterinarian found out why the guinea pig was sick.
What did the veterinarian find out?

The veterinarian found out _____.

(8) The baker told the customer how he bakes the cake.
What did the baker tell the customer?

The baker told the customer _____.

(9) We wondered when the county fair would start.
What did we wonder?

We wondered _____.

(10) The reporter researched where the forest fires began.
What did the reporter research?

The reporter researched _____.

Hint: A noun clause usually begins with the word *that* or a question word such as *why, what, how, where,* or *when.*

Amazing effort.

10 Noun Clauses

Date / /

Name

Level
★ ★

Score

/100

1 Underline the independent clause of each sentence. Then circle the noun clause.

5 points each

(1) My mom was hoping that it would not rain during the football game.

(2) Carla liked to jog where there were no cars.

(3) Everyone agreed that we should get tickets for the fashion show.

(4) The man read where the fireworks would happen.

(5) Anybody could guess what the ending of the book might be.

2 Complete each noun clause with a question word from the box.

5 points each

why	what	how	where	when

(1) Her sister wondered _____ she hadn't thought of the idea herself.

(2) The police officer told the pedestrian _____ the police were doing in the area.

(3) The circus performer asked _____ the circus was traveling to next.

(4) I was surprised _____ my friend snuck up behind me.

(5) The songwriter always describes _____ people fall in love.

3 Write the noun clause of each sentence in the space provided.

5 points each

(1) By the end of the class, you will know why the moon eclipses the sun.

_____

(2) The book will reveal what the character does.

_____

(3) My uncle taught me how he whistles.

_____

(4) A local resident should know where public transportation is located.

_____

(5) I asked my mother when we would pick pumpkins.

_____

(6) They learned how people write computer programs.

_____

(7) The newspaper reported what the government program is about.

_____

(8) The student asked how telescopes work.

_____

(9) His little sister wanted to know why mosquito bites itch.

_____

(10) The man explained that comic books can be valuable.

_____

Exceptional!

Noun Clauses

Date   /   /

Name

Level
★ ★

Score

/100

1 Change each question into a noun clause.

5 points each

(1) Why did the children quarrel?

If you were here earlier, you would know _why the children quarreled_.

(2) What do you do with the herbs?

Read the recipe to find out _____.

(3) How do athletes train for a competition?

The coach explained _____.

(4) Where does the bridge lead?

This map shows _____.

(5) When will the vegetables be ready to harvest?

The *Farmers' Almanac* predicts _____.

2 Answer each question with the noun clause from each sentence.

5 points each

(1) The troop meeting began when everyone had arrived.
When did the troop meeting begin?

_when everyone had arrived_____

(2) She was happy that she was elected class secretary.
Why was she happy?

_____

(3) The governor will discuss how the memorial will look.
What will the governor discuss?

_____

(4) She asked her dentist how a cavity forms.
What did she ask her dentist?

_____

(5) The bus driver told us where he could drop us off.
What did the bus driver tell us?

_____

3 Complete each sentence with a noun clause in your own words. Use the illustrations as a guide.

5 points each

(1) My brother wanted to know _why a porcupine raises its quills_ .

(2) His father looked at the schedule to find out _when_ _____ .

(3) This chapter explains _how_ _____ .

(4) I try to find _where_ _____ .

(5) The younger children wanted to see _what_ _____ .

(6) The sailor told us _how_ _____ .

(7) This imaginative book describes _what_ _____ .

(8) The airplane lands _where_ _____ .

(9) The child asked her parent _why_ _____ .

(10) Our neighbor asked _when_ _____ .

High five!

Level ★★

Date / /

Name

Score

/100

1 Write the dependent clause of each sentence in the space provided.

6 points each

(1) The child ate breakfast before she went to preschool.

_____

(2) The businessman wasn't satisfied until he became a millionaire.

_____

(3) I wanted to write an autobiography if my mother would read it.

_____

(4) The girl was bilingual because her parents spoke different languages.

_____

(5) Jonathan watched his sister until his parents got home.

_____

Don't forget!

An **adverb clause** is a dependent clause that acts as an adverb. An adverb clause modifies or describes a verb, adjective, or adverb.

For example: Tammy asked <u>what was on the menu</u> <u>before they went to the restaurant</u>.

noun clause   adverb clause

2 Complete each sentence with an adverb clause from the box.

5 points each

| when they start to pile up | until he moved |
| after our cat became ill | because he received a diploma |

(1) Joey lived ten minutes away _____.

(2) I rake the leaves _____.

(3) Doug was proud of himself _____.

(4) We rushed to the veterinarian _____.

3 Complete the answer to each question with an adverb clause from the sentence.

5 points each

(1) When our teacher returned, she saw us working.
When did the teacher see us working?

_____ she saw us working.

(2) Because her dog loved her, it followed her everywhere.
Why did the dog follow her everywhere?

_____ it followed her everywhere.

(3) Although the show wasn't popular, Friday's show was sold out.
The show was sold out in spite of what?

_____ Friday's show was sold out.

(4) If the hydrant is opened, gallons of water might pour out.
Why might gallons of water pour out?

_____ gallons of water might pour out.

(5) After the chauffeur dropped her off, the lady thanked him.
When did the lady thank the chauffeur?

_____ the lady thanked him.

(6) She drank water because she was thirsty.
Why did she drink water?

She drank water _____.

(7) Although the flutist was nervous, he played his solo well.
The flutist played his solo well in spite of what?

_____ he played his solo well.

(8) If a bungalow is available, the family will vacation at the beach.
Why might the family vacation at the beach?

_____ the family will vacation there.

(9) Her brother switched hats until he liked his outfit.
For how long did her brother switch hats?

Her brother switched hats _____.

(10) That team won the scavenger hunt because they finished first.
Why did that team win?

That team won _____.

Hint: An adverb clause usually begins with a word like *before*, *after*, *if*, *because*, *although*, etc.

Stupendous.

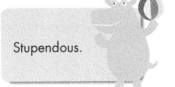

13 Adverb Clauses

1 Underline the independent clause in each sentence. Then circle the adverb clause.

5 points each

(1) I didn't enjoy tennis lessons until I learned to serve.

(2) The scientist did an experiment because he wanted to find a cure.

(3) We could save more trees if people used paper more carefully.

(4) I think of Martin Luther King, Jr. when I think of activism.

(5) Although the horses were strong, they pulled the sleigh slowly.

2 Complete each adverb clause with a word from the box.

5 points each

after	if	before	until	whenever

(1) My aunt was on the brink of tears _____ we found her lost dog.

(2) _____ the scientist's work is discredited, he will have to start over.

(3) My cousin calls a good friend _____ she is feeling sad.

(4) I sprinkled the cheese on the pizza dough _____ my mom had spread the sauce.

(5) _____ the author wrote the book, he did a lot of research.

3   Write the adverb clause of each sentence in the space provided.   5 points each

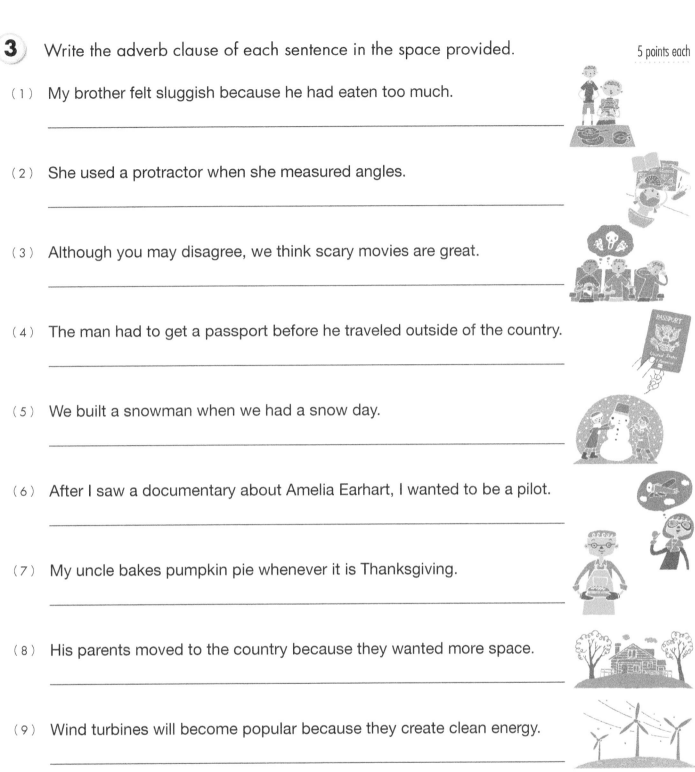

(1) My brother felt sluggish because he had eaten too much.

_____

(2) She used a protractor when she measured angles.

_____

(3) Although you may disagree, we think scary movies are great.

_____

(4) The man had to get a passport before he traveled outside of the country.

_____

(5) We built a snowman when we had a snow day.

_____

(6) After I saw a documentary about Amelia Earhart, I wanted to be a pilot.

_____

(7) My uncle bakes pumpkin pie whenever it is Thanksgiving.

_____

(8) His parents moved to the country because they wanted more space.

_____

(9) Wind turbines will become popular because they create clean energy.

_____

(10) Before she made friends, the new girl felt lonely at her school.

_____

Hint: An adverb clause is often found at the beginning or end of a sentence.

Good for you!

  27

Adverb Clauses

1 Convert each sentence into an adverb clause by adding the word or words in the brackets.

5 points each

(1) I stopped by the gymnasium.   [when]

when I stopped by the gymnasium

(2) Fiction stories are not real.   [because]

_____

(3) The columnist writes about the baseball team.   [if]

_____

(4) That commercial showed Lake Tahoe.   [even though]

_____

(5) She bowled a perfect game.   [after]

_____

2 Answer each question with the adverb clause from each sentence.

5 points each

(1) We carved pumpkins after we decorated for Halloween.
When did we carve pumpkins?

_____

(2) My brother will have an allergic reaction if he eats nuts.
When will my brother have an allergic reaction?

_____

(3) The city created bike lanes because it wanted to reduce traffic.
Why did the city create bike lanes?

_____

(4) The native peoples lived on the island before explorers arrived.
When did native peoples live on the island?

_____

(5) The man had stubble on his face although he shaved that morning.
The man had stubble on his face in spite of what?

_____

3 Complete each sentence with an adverb clause in your own words. Use the illustrations as a guide.

5 points each

(1) We played outside _although_ _____
_____
_____.

(2) I grabbed my lunch _before_ _____
_____
_____.

(3) Her parents said we could go to the movies later _if_ ___
_____
_____.

(4) The student excelled in math _because_ _____
_____
_____.

(5) It was a sunny day _though_ _____
_____
_____.

(6) There was a warning next to the river _because_ _____
_____
_____.

(7) The player bounced the ball off the backboard
before _____
_____.

(8) The song became popular _because_ _____
_____
_____.

(9) My sister set up the nets _while_ _____
_____
_____.

(10) We put signs up around the neighborhood _after_ _____
_____.

You did splendidly!

Adjective Clauses

Date   /   /

Name

Score
/100

1 Write the dependent clause of each sentence in the space provided.

6 points each

(1) This is the office where my father works. _____

(2) These are the clothes that we will donate. _____

(3) The teachers who chaperoned the field trip counted all the students. _____

(4) I am working on an art project that I will enter into a contest. _____

(5) Visiting my aunt's house is a treat that we look forward to. _____

Don't forget!

An **adjective clause** is a dependent clause that acts as an adjective. An adjective clause modifies or describes a noun or pronoun in the sentence, such as the subject.

For example: The students who score 100 percent on the test will get an award.
          subject   adjective clause

2 Complete each sentence with an adjective clause from the box.

5 points each

who are respectful	that has a large screen
that had chickens and goats	that was difficult to win

(1) Our friend showed us a game _____.

(2) Those students _____ are well liked by others.

(3) Her grandmother grew up on a farm _____.

(4) Please purchase a television _____.

3 Complete the answer to each question with an adjective clause from the sentence.

5 points each

(1) Dawn received the prize that recognized academic achievement.
Which prize did Dawn receive?

Dawn received the prize _____.

(2) The boy talked to a doctor who was an asthma expert.
What kind of doctor did the boy talk to?

The boy talked to a doctor _____.

(3) This is the field where the soccer team practices.
Which field is this?

This is the field _____.

(4) We traveled to an island that was inhabited by wild horses.
What sort of island did we travel to?

We traveled to an island _____.

(5) Eve started a campaign that promoted pet adoption.
What kind of campaign did Eve start?

Eve started a campaign _____.

(6) This is the necklace that my grandmother gave to me.
Which necklace is this?

This is the necklace _____.

(7) Musicians who practice regularly will play well.
Who will play well?

Musicians _____ will play well.

(8) We pick apples that are good for baking.
What kind of apples do we pick?

We pick apples _____.

(9) The drama club that Mrs. Alvarez advises went to a play.
Which drama club went to a play?

The drama club _____ went to a play.

(10) The truck driver drove on a path that was mainly rocks and dirt.
What kind of path did the truck driver drive on?

The truck driver drove on a path _____.

Hint: An adjective clause usually begins with a word like *who, that, which, where,* etc.

You're a great example.

16 Adjective Clauses

Date / /   Name

Level ★ ★

Score / 100

1 Underline the independent clause in each sentence. Then circle the adjective clause.

5 points each

(1) The school had a program that encouraged healthy eating.

(2) I ran a 5 kilometer race, which is not long compared to a half marathon.

(3) The costume that I wore last year is too small to fit me now.

(4) We made a haystack, which later fell.

Don't forget!

Begin an adjective clause with *that* when giving information that is essential to the sentence's meaning. Begin an adjective clause with *which* when giving information that is not essential to the sentence's meaning.

---

2 Complete each adjective clause with a word from the box. You can use each word more than once.

6 points each

that	which	where

(1) There were once trees on this land _____ woodpeckers would nest.

(2) My father asked for a screwdriver _____ wasn't so small.

(3) I wear the same jersey number _____ my brother wore.

(4) The hike _____ we took yesterday really tested my endurance.

Hint: Use a comma before an adjective clause that begins with *which*.

(5) The woman bought that dress, _____ is a very popular style.

© *Kumon Publishing Co., Ltd.*

3 Write the adjective clause of each sentence in the space provided.

5 points each

(1)   We created our own board game that required dice.

_____

(2)   That is the building where I take violin lessons.

_____

(3)   She read inside her fort, which she made from sheets.

_____

(4)   They went to the book fair where authors were signing books.

_____

(5)   I filled the bird feeder that attracted robins and sparrows.

_____

(6)   The plumber fixed a leak that wasted a lot of water.

_____

(7)   My school ran a photo contest, which inspired the students.

_____

(8)   We watched the diver who was an excellent athlete.

_____

(9)   The woman, who was a talented face painter, volunteered at the fund-raiser.

_____

(10) Look through the kaleidoscope, where you will see many colors and shapes.

_____

Hint: An adjective clause immediately follows the noun or pronoun that it describes.

Phenomenal!

Adjective Clauses

1 Complete each sentence with the word in the brackets. Then read each sentence aloud.

5 points each

(1) The king, _____ ruled from afar, wanted to raise taxes. [who]

(2) The middle school has a basketball court _____ needs repair. [that]

(3) My youngest cousin is the one _____ dances on pointe. [who]

(4) Rhode Island has a coastline _____ attracts many visitors. [that]

(5) The wet suit was for the man _____ was going scuba diving. [who]

Don't forget!

Begin an adjective clause with *who* when giving information about a person or a group of people. Begin an adjective clause with *that* when giving information about a thing.

2 Complete each sentence with *who* or *that*.

5 points each

(1) The Oregon Trail was filled with families _____ were moving west.

(2) We wash our hands to kill germs _____ make us sick.

(3) The audience members, _____ were applauding, began to stand up.

(4) Our group was led by a volunteer _____ was an expert in forestry.

(5) Guatemala has volcanoes _____ are still active!

3 Complete each sentence with an adjective clause in your own words. Use the illustrations as a guide.

5 points each

(1) Scruffy is a dog _that_ _____ _____ _____.

(2) We compared the shoes, _which_ _____ _____ _____.

(3) She went to the repair shop _where_ _____ _____ _____.

(4) The chorus is for those people _who_ _____ _____ _____.

(5) The group visited a museum _that_ _____ _____ _____.

(6) The boy opened the box, _which_ _____ _____ _____.

(7) The police caught the robbers _who_ _____ _____ _____.

(8) My sister entered a talent contest _that_ _____ _____ _____.

(9) We cheered for the runner _who_ _____ _____ _____.

(10) I want to read a book _that_ _____ _____ _____.

Nice work.

Review
Clauses

Date / /

Name

Level ★ ★

Score /100

1 Complete each noun clause with a word from the box.

5 points each

why	what	how	where	when

(1) The baker would not tell _____ the secret ingredient is.

(2) We found out _____ the train would arrive.

(3) My teacher asked _____ I was late.

(4) The subject of the book is _____ machines work.

(5) The theater is _____ I see many plays.

2 Complete each adverb clause with a word from the box.

5 points each

after	if	before	until	whenever

(1) I sew the skirt together _____ I have cut the fabric.

(2) They will move the party indoors _____ it is too cold outside.

(3) My father exercises outside _____ the weather allows.

(4) I will practice every day _____ my solo performance.

(5) Marty cleared his plate _____ he left the dining room.

3 Complete each adjective clause with a word from the box. You can use each word more than once.

5 points each

who	that	which	where

(1) The test _____ we took last week was not difficult.

(2) That is the farm _____ my grandfather grew up.

(3) My brother saw a musician _____ is very popular now.

(4) Schoolchildren _____ eat a good breakfast concentrate better in class.

(5) We biked along a trail, _____ was more difficult than we thought.

4 Underline the independent clause in each sentence. Circle the dependent clause. Then write the type of dependent clause in the space provided.

5 points each

(1) The cat sleeps whenever she can.   _____

(2) I wondered how a cactus can live for so long without water.   _____

(3) I will take a bus if the subway isn't running.   _____

(4) The vase that he broke was inexpensive.   _____

(5) She asked what the book was about.   _____

You're fantastic!

Three-Paragraph Essay
Review

19

Level ★★

Date / /

Name

Score /100

1 Read the paragraph. Complete the topic with words from the passage.   10 points each

(1)

My best friend and I are alike in some ways and not alike in others. She enjoys playing the cello, while I enjoy playing sports. She likes to read historical fiction novels, but I really like mysteries. However, we became best friends because we make each other laugh.

Comparing and contrasting ___best friends___

(2)

If you were born in ancient Greece, you wouldn't use a pencil and paper—and you certainly wouldn't use a computer! At that time, a student wrote on a wooden tablet covered in wax. The student used a pointed stick called a stylus to scratch letters in the wax. The student used the blunt edge to rub letters out.

Writing utensils in _____

(3)

To plan a luau party, first set a date and invite your friends. Then, buy balloons, hibiscus flowers, grass skirts, and leis for decorations and costumes. When your friends arrive, place a lei around each person's neck and say "Aloha!" You can serve coconut water, baked mahimahi, and pineapple.

How to _____

(4)

Did you know that Pocahontas was one of the first Native Americans to visit England? She traveled there in a small, wooden sailing ship with her son and her husband, John Rolfe. Pocahontas was very well liked in England, and many people wanted to see her. She even met King James I.

Pocahontas's trip to _____

(5)

Getting a good night's rest can help you when you're awake. Many studies show that taking even a brief nap can boost your memory and sharpen your thinking skills. Getting enough sleep can also make you feel more optimistic and ready to face your challenges—something every student needs!

Why it is important to get a _____

2 Complete the paragraph with a main idea from the box.

20 points for completion

- Underneath New York City's spectacular skyscrapers is the equally impressive subway system.
- Expressways are a tremendous feat of engineering and problem solving.
- The New York City subway system was made possible by the invention of electric motors.

_____

_____ On October 27, 1904, 28 subway stations opened to help move the swelling population around the growing city. Today, there are 468 stations. On an average weekday, 5.3 million people ride the subway. More than 6,280 subway cars run over approximately 660 miles of track. Laid end to end, those tracks would reach from New York to Chicago.

3 Write the main idea of each paragraph in the space provided.

15 points each

(1)

After a panda cub is born, it is entirely blind for more than a month. It has only a thin coat of fur and cannot walk for the first seventy-five days of its life. It depends on its mother for everything. Panda cubs are extremely fragile infants.

_____

_____

(2)

Coral reefs are important and must be protected. Coral reefs tell us a lot about water quality and environmental changes. Coral reefs protect coastlines and beaches from erosion. Last, coral reefs are an ecosystem for diverse plants and fish. Coral reefs are at risk due to global warming.

_____

_____

This is challenging!

Three-Paragraph Essay
Review

20

Level ★ ★

Date / /

Name

Score /100

1 Read the paragraph. Then complete the chart.

10 points each

Many people believe that the one-dollar bill should be part of the United States' past. Legislators are considering ending production of the one-dollar bill and replacing it with the one-dollar coin, and it just might benefit the country if they did so. According to the Government Accountability Office, the move to dollar coins would save the government $5.6 billion over thirty years. Why? Paper money only lasts an average of three and a half years and then must be replaced. Coins last a lot longer. Many other countries have coins for smaller amounts of money, like the one-euro coin in Europe. Companies that provide metal sheets will benefit from the demand for metal. Also, vending machine companies and public transportation agencies support the substitution because the coins are easier to use in vending and ticketing machines.

Main Idea	(1) _____ _____
Supporting Details	(2) Using dollar coins would save _____ over thirty years.
	(3) _____ only lasts an average of three and a half years, but coins last longer.
	(4) Other _____ have coins for smaller amounts of money.
	(5) Different businesses will benefit from the change, such as companies that provide _____, vending machine companies, and _____.

2 Complete the passage with a main idea and transition sentences from the box. 10 points each

---

- That historical change is affecting schools and communities today.
- Sadly, it wasn't until the 1970s that women in the United States would lobby for such a commemoration.
- Every March, the United States celebrates Women's History Month, but it wasn't always that way.
- How did this change come about?
- While Women's History Week was a victory, it was just the beginning.

---

(1)_____

_____ Although women accomplished many feats throughout history, the U.S. public didn't focus on women's achievements until recently. (2)_____

_____

The idea grew out of activism by women around the world in the early twentieth century. On March 19, 1911, the first International Women's Day was held in several countries. The event focused on women's rights and issues. (3)_____

_____

In 1978, a school district in California began Women's History Week to promote teaching history that focused on female pioneers. They chose a week in March to include International Women's Day. It became so popular that Congress passed a resolution in 1981 to encourage the entire country to celebrate the week. (4)_____

_____

As more people began to study women's history, its popularity grew. With much popular support, a group of women asked Congress in 1987 to expand the celebration. That same year, Congress declared March to be National Women's History Month. (5)_____

_____

_____

Now, every March, schools and communities mark Women's History Month with activities and lessons that focus on how women have shaped U.S. history. The next challenge for women is ensuring that their history is taught all year-round.

Hint: A transition sentence helps the reader move from one paragraph to the next.

Keep up the good work!

41

Three-Paragraph Essay
Review

Date   /   /

Name

---

1 Complete the three-paragraph essay with sentences from the box.

10 points each

- Though this plan is extreme, there are many benefits to this idea.
- Lastly, biking, which is a great form of exercise, would be encouraged.
- If I could plan a town, I would allow only public transportation and bicycles.
- In closing, if I could plan a town, I would organize it around public transportation and bicycles.
- The roads would have less traffic, and people could commute easily.

---

(1)_____

_____ By excluding individual cars and trucks, my town would

have less traffic, be environmentally friendly, and also be home to healthier people. This one

choice could affect my town in many positive ways.

(2)_____

_____ By using only public transportation such as subways, trams, and buses,

we could reduce much of the pollution that motor vehicles create. (3)_____

_____ There wouldn't even be a need for parking lots! That space

could be used for parks and recreation. The reduction of

pollution would mean better air for the townspeople to

breathe. (4)_____

_____

_____

(5)_____

_____

_____ Less pollution, less

traffic, and healthy townspeople would make it a great place

to live.

Hint: A three-paragraph essay includes an introductory paragraph, a body or supporting paragraph, and a conclusion.

---

2 Complete the chart with phrases and sentences from the box.

10 points each

- The debate over using animals in movies is complicated,
- Animals should be used in films, but only with strict regulation.
- They perform important roles, can educate the public, and are adored by audiences.
- In the 1940s, cruel and hazardous practices used with animal actors were prohibited.
- not all animals can enjoy a good life outside the wild.

Topic: Should animal actors be used in films?

⬇

Main Idea:

(1)_____

⬇   ⬇   ⬇

Supporting Details 1:	**Supporting Details 2:**	**Supporting Details 3:**
• (2)_____ _____ _____ _____	• However, (3)_____ _____ _____	• Animals have been wonderful additions to films throughout movie history. • (4)_____ _____ _____ _____
• Now the American Humane Association monitors movie productions to make sure animals are safe and these practices don't occur.	• Therefore, more limitations should be enforced, and more animation and digital technology should be used instead.	

⬇   ⬇   ⬇

Conclusion: (5)_____
but overall, it is important to do what is best for the animals.

Hint: You can use a chart to brainstorm and plan your essay before writing it.

You are clever!

Three-Paragraph Essay
Review

22

Level ★★

Date / /

Name

Score /100

1 Complete the chart with phrases and sentences from the box.

10 points each

- In conclusion, nature has a lot of astonishing powers that can create strange, damaging, and exciting events.
- One Serbian town even experienced a frog shower one day!
- If it is pushed by strong winds, this snow can roll into logs, which are called "snow rollers."
- Nature can be incredibly powerful and perform many destructive and dazzling feats.
- Keep an eye out during a thunderstorm for "ball lightning."

Topic: The power of nature

Main Idea:

(1)_____

_____

Supporting Details 1:

- (2)_____

_____

_____

- Ball lightning is a glowing ball of lightning that is roughly the size of your head.
- It appears to drop down to the ground, travel, and then dart up into the air.

Supporting Details 2:

- Waterspouts and tornadoes suck up whatever they come across.
- If they happen to cross over a lake, they can carry water and fish a long way away.
- (3)_____

_____

_____

Supporting Details 3:

- Nature can even make its own snowballs.
- When wet snow falls on ice, the snow won't stick to the ground.
- (4)_____

_____

_____

_____

Conclusion: (5)_____

_____

2 Complete the chart in your own words based on the given topic.

50 points for completion

Topic: Good neighbors

Main Idea:

Good neighbors are people who are _____

_____

Supporting Details 1:

* _____
  _____
  _____
  _____

* _____
  _____
  _____
  _____

* _____
  _____
  _____
  _____

Supporting Details 2:

* _____
  _____
  _____
  _____

* _____
  _____
  _____
  _____

* _____
  _____
  _____
  _____

Supporting Details 3:

* _____
  _____
  _____
  _____

* _____
  _____
  _____
  _____

* _____
  _____
  _____
  _____

Conclusion: In conclusion, _____

_____

_____

_____

_____

Your writing rocks!

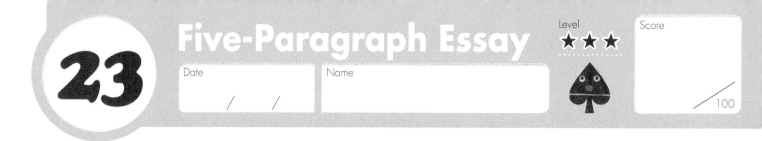

Five-Paragraph Essay

23

Level
★ ★ ★

Score

/100

Date / /

Name

1 Read the five-paragraph essay. Then label each excerpt or phrase with a description from the box. You can use each label more than once.

20 points each

In the United States, Election Day occurs every four years on the first Tuesday in November, but in some states, voting can start more than a month in advance. Thirty-four states and Washington, D.C. allow early voting in person and/or by mail. The amount of people who are early voters is climbing—from 16 percent in 2000 to 33 percent in 2008. Due to its rising popularity, early voting is changing the way presidential campaigns spend money and address issues. However, counting the results of early voting is still an unreliable way to forecast winners.

As early voting becomes more widespread, campaigns must figure out how best to spend their money. In states that allow voting only on Election Day, it makes sense to increase advertising as the date draws closer, so the candidate's message is fresh in people's minds. In early voting states, campaigns must make sure that their advertising reaches people for a longer period of time (from when early voting starts until Election Day), which makes the total cost greater.

Similarly, campaigns direct their messages differently in early voting states. Campaigns will research the people most likely to vote early and focus on issues that those people care about. Once the majority of those people have voted, candidates can target voters who are still undecided or are reluctant to vote. While campaigns spend a lot of money and energy on early voting, the results of early voting are not always the best indicator of who will win.

History has shown that studying early voting is not a reliable way to determine who will win an election. Many campaigns and journalists will research how many people from each political party have requested early voting ballots and use this information to help predict the outcome of the election. However, the number of early voters does not tell the full story. For example, in 2004, John Kerry had more early votes in Iowa than George W. Bush. Nonetheless, Bush won the state on the final count.

Election Day may be the most dramatic day of presidential campaigns, but voting can start a long time beforehand. Campaigns spend differently and send different messages to states that have early voting. Still, early voting is not a reliable way to judge the outcome of the election. Early voting may be getting more popular, but an election's outcome still isn't fixed until Election Day.

A	topic	**C**	transition
B	supporting detail	**D**	conclusion

(1) _____ Early voting and predicting election outcomes

(2) _____ Early voting may be getting more popular, but an election's outcome still isn't fixed until Election Day.

(3) _____ For example, in 2004, John Kerry had more early votes in Iowa than George W. Bush. Nonetheless, Bush won the state on the final count.

(4) _____ While campaigns spend a lot of money and energy on early voting, the results of early voting are not always the best indicator of who will win.

(5) _____ Thirty-four states and Washington, D.C. allow early voting in person and/or by mail.

Don't forget!

A **five-paragraph essay** is a piece of writing that is organized into five paragraphs.
The **introductory paragraph** is the first paragraph. It states the main idea of the essay.
The **body** or the **supporting paragraphs** are the second, third, and fourth paragraphs.
They give details on the topic and evidence to support the main idea. The **conclusion** is the
fifth paragraph. It summarizes the essay and reinforces the ideas given in the introductory
paragraph and body.

I'm impressed!

Five-Paragraph Essay
Choosing a Topic

24

Level ★ ★ ★

Score

Date   /   /

Name

/100

1 Complete each brainstorming list of essay topics in your own words.

14 points each

(1)
> **My favorite...**
> sport
> band
> clothing item
> _____
> _____

(2)
> **If I were president, I would...**
> make college mandatory
> reduce pollution
> build better roads and bridges
> _____
> _____

(3)
> **Once I was afraid of _____, but now I'm not.**
> trying out for a sports team
> speaking in public
> not knowing anyone at a party
> _____
> _____

(4)
> **If I could volunteer, I would...**
> work at an animal shelter
> help out at a home for the elderly
> fund-raise for my local firehouse
> _____
> _____

(5)
> **I would like to visit...**
> Australia
> England
> Mexico
> _____
> _____

2 Brainstorm as many main ideas as you can for each topic. Circle the topic with the most ideas. If you have the same number of ideas for all topics, circle all three. 10 points each

(1)

My best friend...
is a loyal friend
makes me laugh
_____
_____
_____

Trying new things is...
scary
exciting
_____
_____
_____

Best ways to study...
in the library
rereading class notes
_____
_____
_____

(2)

Why recycle?
to save resources
to stop pollution
_____
_____
_____

The best books are...
funny
heartwarming
_____
_____
_____

Good sportsmanship is...
being a good teammate
playing fairly
_____
_____
_____

(3)

If you get lost...
call home
find a police officer
_____
_____
_____

Good nutrition can...
fuel your day
keep you healthy
_____
_____
_____

Life in outer space...
is probable
will find us
_____
_____
_____

Hint: Choose a topic that inspires many ideas. If a topic is too narrow, you may run out of ideas to write about. A good topic to write about will have three main ideas and some supporting details.

Outstanding!

Five-Paragraph Essay
Topic Sentences

Level ★★★

Date / /

Name

Score
/100

(25)

1 Read each introductory paragraph topic sentence. Write the essay's main idea and the supporting paragraphs' main ideas.

10 points each

(1) Woodpeckers can knock their bills into trees repeatedly because they have dense skulls, small brains, and little fluid in their heads so their brains can't slosh around.

Essay's main idea:

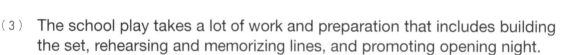

Supporting paragraphs' main ideas:

① Woodpeckers have _____.

② Woodpeckers have _____.

③ Woodpeckers have _____.

(2) Regular exercise has many health benefits besides fitness; it also boosts memory, improves moods, and reduces stress.

Essay's main idea:

_____

Supporting paragraphs' main ideas:

① Exercise _____.

② Exercise _____.

③ Exercise _____.

(3) The school play takes a lot of work and preparation that includes building the set, rehearsing and memorizing lines, and promoting opening night.

Essay's main idea:

_____

Supporting paragraphs' main ideas:

① The students must _____.

② The students must _____.

③ The students must _____.

> ## Don't forget!
>
> A **topic sentence** is a sentence that describes what an essay or paragraph is mostly about. The introductory paragraph of a five-paragraph essay usually begins with a topic sentence that states the three main ideas that will appear in the body. Each supporting paragraph in the body will also include a topic sentence elaborating its main idea.

2 Read each supporting paragraph topic sentence. Write the essay's topic and the supporting paragraph's main idea.

14 points each

(1) My best friend is so generous that she shares her treat with me whenever I forget mine.

Topic: My best friend

Essay's main idea:

My best friend is generous.

Supporting paragraph's main idea:

She shares her treat with me.

(2) One of the best ways to study is to read the notes you took in class.

Topic: _____

Essay's main idea:

_____

Supporting paragraph's main idea:

_____

(3) In sports, good sportsmanship means playing fairly.

Topic: _____

Essay's main idea:

_____

Supporting paragraph's main idea:

_____

(4) One reason to recycle is to save precious resources.

Topic: _____

Essay's main idea:

_____

Supporting paragraph's main idea:

_____

(5) If you are lost, get help by finding a police officer to assist you.

Topic: _____

Essay's main idea:

_____

Supporting paragraph's main idea:

_____

Remarkable!

Five-Paragraph Essay
Introductory Paragraph

26

Level
★ ★ ★

Score

/100

Date   /   /

Name

1 Complete each introductory paragraph by writing a topic sentence with the essay topic and main idea and the supporting paragraphs' main ideas.

25 points each

(1) **Topic:** Wolves / **Essay's main idea:** Wolves should be protected in Wyoming.
Supporting paragraphs' main ideas:
① There are few of them left.
② They improve their ecosystem's well-being.
③ Their actions help other animals.

> There are many reasons why wolves should be
> protected in Wyoming
>
> _____
>
> _____
>
> Many people fear wolves. However, while wolves may have a bad reputation, they do contribute to the environment, so action must be taken.

(2) **Topic:** Referees / **Essay's main idea:** Referees play an important role in sports.
Supporting paragraphs' main ideas:
① They ensure fair play.
② They settle disputes.
③ They keep games moving quickly.

> _____
>
> _____
>
> _____
>
> Could you imagine any major-league sport without referees? Although some people may disagree with specific calls referees make, having them at games gives both teams a fair chance to win.

Don't forget!

An **introductory paragraph** in a five-paragraph essay includes a topic sentence with three main ideas, a sentence that "hooks" the reader, and a transition sentence that leads the reader to a supporting paragraph. The transition sentence generally leads to a supporting paragraph about the first main idea listed in the topic sentence. The introductory paragraph is like an outline for the reader.

2 Write each introductory paragraph with the information provided. Include a topic sentence, a hook, and a transition sentence.

25 points each

(1) **Topic:** Droughts / **Essay's main idea:** Droughts greatly affect the environment.
   Supporting paragraphs' main ideas:
   ① Droughts ruin food crops.
   ② Droughts increase the risk of wildfires.
   ③ Droughts limit drinking water.
   Hook information: While most weather patterns last for a short time, droughts can last for many years.

_____

_____

_____

_____

_____

(2) **Topic:** Earthquakes / **Essay's main idea:** You can lead an earthquake drill.
   Supporting paragraphs' main ideas:
   ① Make a plan in case of earthquakes.
   ② Teach your class or group what to do.
   ③ Practice.
   Hook information: Although earthquakes typically occur in certain areas, they can happen anywhere and at any time.

_____

_____

_____

_____

_____

Don't forget!

To "hook" the reader into your essay, include a sentence or two that has a surprising fact, a quotation, a definition, or perhaps an interesting anecdote that relates to the topic.

You're a champ!

Five-Paragraph Essay
Supporting Paragraphs

Level ★ ★ ★

Score

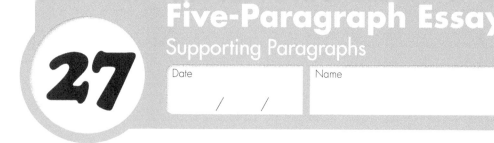

27

Date
/ /

Name

/100

1 Complete each supporting paragraph with a topic sentence from the box.

15 points each

- Besides spurring the economy with innovation, space exploration creates jobs.
- Furthermore, more space exploration leads to innovations in science and technology, which is an essential part of a strong economy.
- Governments should spend more money to explore space because this exploration gets people interested in the sciences.

---

(1)

_____
_____
_____ Space travel excites people and encourages a culture that values science, technology, and innovation, which often leads to scientific progress. For example, the Mars rover Curiosity discovered water on Mars, which sparked interest in the nature of Mars and in life on other planets.

(2)

_____
_____
_____ For example, cell phones and the Global Positioning System (GPS) were spin-offs of NASA's work. Consumer electronics and other technology originally created for space programs can propel a country's economy.

(3)

_____
_____
_____ Space programs create high-paying and high-tech positions. Furthermore, space exploration creates business opportunities for companies that supply materials and services. Therefore, jobs are created in many different businesses as a result of space exploration.

Don't forget!

A **supporting paragraph** helps explain, describe, or elaborate on one of the main ideas in the introductory paragraph's topic sentence. Each supporting paragraph should include a topic sentence and sentences with supporting details, facts, and examples.

2 Complete each supporting paragraph with a sentence from the box.

- He coined more than one thousand words, many of which are still frequently used.
- His work is read in at least eighty languages, including Chinese, Armenian, Bengali, and many more.
- For example, in *A Midsummer Night's Dream*, four separate plots interact and end with a happy marriage.

(1)

William Shakespeare stands out as an author because of his broad appeal. Although he wrote his plays and poems in the late sixteenth to early seventeenth century, his work continues to be read and performed, and not only in English-speaking countries. Shakespeare is the most translated author ever. _____

_____

_____

(2)

Besides the fact that Shakespeare's stories have universal appeal, Shakespeare is also highly regarded because of his clever writing and wordplay. _____

_____

These words include *rival*, *madcap*, *radiance*, *lackluster*, and *schoolboy*. Yet his inventiveness did not stop with words.

(3)

Shakespeare is also considered one of the most important authors of all time because many credit him with inventing the genre of romantic comedy with overlapping plots. We know the format well today—a lighthearted tone, young love overcoming difficulty, different styles of humor, and a happy ending. _____

_____

_____

Your writing rules!

28

Score

/ 100

Date
/ /

Name

1 Read each supporting paragraph topic sentence. Then put a check mark next to the detail that supports the topic sentence best.

15 points each

(1) Dogs should not be fed chocolate.

_____ ⓐ Chocolate contains a chemical that can make a dog very sick.

_____ ⓑ Dogs like chocolate even though they should not eat it.

_____ ⓒ If your pet is sick, ask an adult to call a veterinarian.

(2) Some doctors think that milk is not the best source of calcium.

_____ ⓐ Many parents don't want to take milk off of school menus.

_____ ⓑ Calcium keeps bones and teeth healthy.

_____ ⓒ Doctors argue that milk is high in sugar, fat, and animal protein, which can be unhealthy.

(3) Trolley companies built amusement parks at the end of trolley lines to attract weekend and evening riders.

_____ ⓐ The first upside-down roller coaster was built at the end of the nineteenth century.

_____ ⓑ Coney Island is a well-known example of an amusement park that was built at the end of a trolley line.

_____ ⓒ Most trolleys, or "trams," use electricity today.

Don't forget!

Supporting details explain, describe, or elaborate on the supporting paragraph's main idea. Supporting details can include facts, arguments, anecdotes, definitions, research, and examples.

2   Read each topic sentence. Brainstorm two supporting details.

15 points each

(1)   Schools should take students on more field trips.
- Some children learn better with hands-on experiences.
- Field trips bring topics to life.

_____

_____

_____

(2)   Don't judge a person by the way he or she looks.
- Beauty does not determine whether you are a good person or not.
- Beauty often does not last.

_____

_____

_____

3   Choose one of the above topics, and write a supporting paragraph with the topic sentence and supporting details.

25 points for completion

_____

_____

_____

_____

_____

_____

_____

_____

_____

Nicely done.

Five-Paragraph Essay
Transition Sentences

29

Date / /

Name

Level ★★★

Score / 100

1 Read the two topic sentences. Then put a check mark next to the sentence that transitions best from one topic sentence to the other.

10 points each

(1) Many records were broken at the 2012 Summer Olympic Games.
More women competed than ever before.

_____ ⓐ While new world records are an exciting feat, another landmark change happened at the Olympics.

_____ ⓑ U.S. women earned twenty-nine gold medals.

_____ ⓒ The women were responsible for some of the most memorable moments of the games.

(2) To make a decision, some people may make a list of pros and cons.
In order to decide, some people may ask advice from experts.

_____ ⓐ Emotions can often get in the way of people's good judgment.

_____ ⓑ Use two separate sheets of paper—one for pros and one for cons.

_____ ⓒ Even with a pros and cons list, people can still be unsure.

(3) Droughts have been damaging many crops across the nation.
Experts predict an increase in the cost of poultry.

_____ ⓐ Droughts are long periods of dry weather.

_____ ⓑ The increase in the cost of crops and poultry will be roughly 10 percent.

_____ ⓒ Due to the lack of crops, farmers are finding it more expensive to feed their livestock.

Don't forget!

Transition sentences connect paragraphs and lead the reader from one idea to another. Sometimes a transition sentence is combined with a topic sentence.

---

2 Read each pair of topic sentences. Then write a transition sentence or phrase to lead the reader from one idea to the other.

14 points each

(1) Scientists discovered a new species of monkey in central Africa.
Many people believe there are still new species to discover.

As a result of such recent discoveries, some wonder what else is unknown.

(2) Our school holds an annual contest for healthy lunch recipes.
Students invent creative, delicious, and wholesome dishes.

_____

_____

_____

(3) Our local team won the Little League National Championships.
It will represent the United States in the Little League Baseball World Series.

_____

_____

_____

(4) Being a veterinarian is difficult when you can't cure an animal.
Being a veterinarian is wonderful because you meet different animals.

_____

_____

_____

(5) Arthur Ashe was the first African American male tennis player to win a Grand Slam title at the U.S. Open.
Arthur Ashe Kids' Day celebrates Arthur Ashe's legacy.

_____

_____

_____

Hint: Many transition sentences include words or phrases such as *furthermore, in addition, as a result, consequently, on the other hand, nevertheless, to put it differently, next, meanwhile,* and *with this in mind.*

You did it!

Five-Paragraph Essay
Conclusion

30

Level
★ ★ ★

Score

/100

Date   /   /

Name

1 Read the conclusion. Fill in the chart.

8 points each

> In summary, carbon monoxide poisoning is preventable. Have all your gas-, oil-, and coal-burning appliances checked by a technician every year. Another important step is to install a battery-operated carbon monoxide detector in your home and to check the batteries often. Also, seek medical help if you feel dizzy, light-headed, or nauseous. In conclusion, these three steps can help you prevent carbon monoxide poisoning.

Essay's main idea:

(1) _____

Supporting paragraphs' main ideas:

(2) _____

_____

(3) _____

_____

(4) _____

_____

Concluding sentence:

(5) _____

_____

Don't forget!

A **conclusion** restates the essay's topic and main idea, summarizes the main ideas of the supporting paragraphs, and brings the essay to a close.

2 Use each chart to write a conclusion. Restate the essay's topic and main idea, state the supporting paragraphs' main ideas, and write a concluding sentence. 30 points each

(1)

> **Essay's main idea:**
> - In the United States, free speech is a recognized human right.
>
> **Supporting paragraphs' main ideas:**
> - The First Amendment states that all citizens are entitled to freedom of speech.
> - Recently, people have been applying the ideals of freedom of speech to the Internet and social media.
> - The boundaries of free speech have been tested in many court cases, but free speech is still a fundamental right.

_____

_____

_____

_____

_____

_____

(2)

> **Essay's main idea:**
> - You can promote peace in your day-to-day life.
>
> **Supporting paragraphs' main ideas:**
> - Be tolerant of others even if you don't always agree or get along.
> - Forgive yourself and others for mistakes, and make sure errors are not repeated.
> - Treat others as you would like to be treated.

_____

_____

_____

_____

_____

_____

Hint: Many conclusions include the following words or phrases: *in conclusion, in short, in summary, to summarize, finally, in other words, as a result, consequently, for this reason, therefore,* and *thus.*

I conclude that you are smart!

Five-Paragraph Essay
Outlining

31

Level ★ ★ ★

Score

Date / /

Name

/ 100

1 Complete the outline with the phrases from the box.

10 points each

Supporting detail   Main idea of supporting paragraph 3
Restatement of introduction's topic sentence
Concluding sentence   Topic sentence of supporting paragraph 1

Introduction

I. Topic Sentence
   A. Main idea of supporting paragraph 1
   B. Main idea of supporting paragraph 2

   C. (1)_____

Body

II. (2)_____
   A. Supporting detail
   B. Supporting detail
   C. Supporting detail

III. Topic sentence of supporting paragraph 2
   A. Supporting detail

   B. (3)_____
   C. Supporting detail

IV. Topic sentence of supporting paragraph 3
   A. Supporting detail
   B. Supporting detail
   C. Supporting detail

Conclusion

V. (4)_____
   A. Summary of supporting paragraph 1
   B. Summary of supporting paragraph 2
   C. Summary of supporting paragraph 3

   D. (5)_____

Don't forget!

An **outline** is a detailed plan for an essay. A five-paragraph essay outline should include the essential parts of the introduction, body, and conclusion. You can also use an outline to brainstorm ideas for your essay.

2 Complete the outline with the sentences from the box. 10 points each

- Nevertheless, kids should recognize how their peer group influences them.
- Peer pressure is harmful if kids' peers make unhealthy choices.
- Wearing certain clothes to try to fit in can harm self-esteem.
- Peers can prompt positive actions, too.
- Peer pressure can be good or bad, and kids should be mindful of its impact.

Introduction
I. Peer pressure can be harmful or beneficial, and kids should be aware of its effects.

    A. (1)_____

    B. Peer pressure is beneficial if kids are pushed to do positive things.

    C. Kids can make good choices if they understand peer pressure.

Body
II. On the negative side, peer pressure can push kids to do things that are bad for them or things they don't want to do.

    A. Smoking cigarettes often starts because of peer pressure.

    B. (2)_____

    C. Peers may encourage bad behavior, like bullying or teasing.

III. On the positive side, a peer group's positive actions and attitudes can pursuade individual kids to do a lot of good.

    A. Sports team players tend to push each other to improve.

    B. Groups that volunteer encourage others to join in their goals.

    C. Peers that excel in school act as good role models for friends.

IV. (3)_____

    A. Being aware of peer pressure helps kids decide if it is positively or negatively affecting them.

    B. A person must think for himself or herself.

    C. Being an individual also makes a person special.

Conclusion
V. (4)_____

    A. Peers can influence kids in a negative way.

    B. (5)_____

    C. Either way, kids should be aware of peer pressure and its consequences.

    D. By being aware of the impact of peer pressure, kids will choose their friends more wisely.

You are well organized!

32

1 Read the introductory paragraph. Then complete each exercise.

25 points each

> Skiing and snowbording are great winter sports because you can spend time outside, see beutiful landscapes and keep healthy during the winter months. There is even a month deddicated to skiing and snowboarding—January is Learn to Ski and Snowboard Month? Janary may be a time when most peple stay indoor, but it a wonderful month to head into the great outdoors.

(1) List the misspelled words with the correct spelling in the space provided.

_____   _____

_____   _____

_____   _____

(2) Correct the punctuation in the following excerpts. Use correct spelling as well.

ⓐ Skiing and snowbording are great winter sports because you can spend time outside, see beutiful landscapes and keep healthy during the winter months.

_____

_____

_____

_____

ⓑ There is even a month deddicated to skiing and snowboarding—January is Learn to Ski and Snowboard Month?

_____

_____

_____

Don't forget!

Your five-paragraph essay must have
- ✔ all five paragraphs
- ✔ proper grammar
- ✔ correct spelling
- ✔ correct punctuation
- ✔ correct formatting
- ✔ clear and concise sentences

(3) Correct the grammar and spelling of the excerpt.

Janary may be a time when most peple stay indoor, but it a wonderful month to head into the great outdoors.

_____

_____

_____

(4) Check the items that were correct in the paragraph on page 64.

_____ ⓐ proper grammer

_____ ⓑ correct spelling

_____ ⓒ correct punctuation

_____ ⓓ correct formatting, such as indentation

_____ ⓔ the introductory paragraph has a topic sentence

_____ ⓕ the topic sentence has three main ideas

_____ ⓖ the introductory paragraph has a transition sentence

_____ ⓗ the introductory paragraph has a hook

Wonderful work!

33

Five-Paragraph Essay

Level
★★★

Score

Date
/ /

Name

/100

1 Choose a topic from the box. Then complete the outline in your own words.

50 points for completion

If I were principal for a day…	I can't wait until I can…
The best kind of weather is…	My favorite place is…

Introduction

I. _____

    A. _____

    B. _____

    C. _____

Body

II. _____

    A. _____

    B. _____

    C. _____

III. _____

    A. _____

    B. _____

    C. _____

IV. _____

    A. _____

    B. _____

    C. _____

Conclusion

V. _____

    A. _____

    B. _____

    C. _____

    D. _____

Hint: If you are having difficulty, review pages 62 and 63.

2 Use the outline on page 66 to write a five-paragraph essay.

50 points for completion

That's writing worth reading!

34 Review

Date   /   /

Name

1 Complete the direct-speech sentences based on the illustration.   5 points each

"You have ten more minutes of recess."

"I'll race you to the water fountain."

"Did you study for the science test?"

"You're on!"

"Of course!"

James   Angela   Eve   Mitch

(1) The teacher said _____

(2) James said _____

(3) Angela said _____

(4) Eve asked _____

(5) Mitch replied _____

2 Complete the indirect-speech sentences based on the illustration.   5 points each

"The plane will depart on time."

"I'm excited for our trip."

"Let's look at our itinerary."

"I'm afraid of flying!"

"Flying is very safe."

(1) The flight attendant said _____.

(2) The woman said _____.

(3) Her husband said _____.

(4) The boy said _____.

(5) The sister suggested _____.

3 Underline the independent clause in each sentence. Circle the dependent clause. Then write whether it is a noun clause, an adverb clause, or an adjective clause. 5 points each

(1) We drank cider after we picked apples. _____

(2) This treasure map showed where the pirates had to go. _____

(3) We went to swim practice before we did our homework. _____

(4) I asked the expert who knew a lot about it. _____

(5) We bought tickets, which were for the wrong date. _____

(6) I go hiking whenever the weather is good. _____

(7) The boy wondered what walking on the moon is like. _____

(8) The teacher will give a quiz if we finish this chapter today. _____

(9) This is the classroom where we do science experiments. _____

(10) He asked what my essay was about. _____

You're almost at the finish line!

1 Choose a topic from the box. Then complete the outline in your own words.

50 points for completion

| My greatest accomplishment | A month without computers |
| An awesome invention | The most influential person in my life |

Introduction

I. _____

    A. _____

    B. _____

    C. _____

Body

II. _____

    A. _____

    B. _____

    C. _____

III. _____

    A. _____

    B. _____

    C. _____

IV. _____

    A. _____

    B. _____

    C. _____

Conclusion

V. _____

    A. _____

    B. _____

    C. _____

    D. _____

Congratulations!
You did it!

1 Punctuation: Review   pp 2,3

1 (1) , / , / ,   (2) , / , / ,   (3) , / ,   (4) , / ,   (5) , / , / ,

2 (1) I like eggplant, mushrooms, and green beans.
 (2) The first aid kit has bandages, alcohol wipes, and adhesive tape.
 (3) My brother doesn't play the piano, guitar, or violin.
 (4) People, chimpanzees, and dolphins are mammals.
 (5) He doesn't have a French, Japanese, or Peruvian stamp.

3 (1) Our room is finished, but the paint must dry.
 (2) The students walked to school, and they played during recess.
 (3) We had fun at the park, so we asked if we could go again.
 (4) The snow fell quickly, yet it melted when it hit the ground.
 (5) The couple wanted to play tennis, but the court was wet.

4 (1) , but there weren't any good ones playing
 (2) , and it is the symbol of the United States
 (3) , or they could ride their bicycles
 (4) , yet they are strong for their size
 (5) , so raccoons won't get inside it

2 Punctuation: Review   pp 4,5

1 (1) , / " / ! / "   (2) " / , / "   (3) " / ? / "
 (4) " / , / "   (5) , / " / ? / "

2 (1) , / .   (2) ,   (3) ?   (4) , / .   (5) , / ?

3 (1) The art teacher said, "Clean your brushes."
 (2) I told Allan, "Meet me when you finish your chores."
 (3) Our coach yelled, "Defense!"
 (4) The woman asked, "May I please have a napkin?"
 (5) The announcer said, "The score is two to one."
 (6) A flight attendant told us, "Please buckle your seat belts."
 (7) Our conductor exclaimed, "That was wonderful!"
 (8) The mail carrier said, "This is not enough postage."
 (9) "May I go to Angela's house?" Tamra asked.
 (10) My science teacher said, "Blood moves through the blood vessels."

3 Direct / Indirect Speech   pp 6,7

1 (1) , "Why do we recycle?"
 (2) , "We recycle to reuse materials."
 (3) , "We recycle to create less trash."
 (4) , "We recycle to protect animals."

2 (1) that her project is about irrigation
 (2) that she would like to see it in action
 (3) that Mr. Stevens helped him a lot
 (4) that Jack should be very proud / that he should be very proud

3 (1) D   (2) I   (3) I   (4) D   (5) I

4 (1) The queen said, "I love this book!"
 (2) Our cousins told us that Thanksgiving dinner would be at their house.
 (3) My father asked, "Did you finish your chores?"
 (4) I heard someone ask if the store would be closing soon.
 (5) The radio announcer said, "Snow is likely all day tomorrow."

4 Complex Sentences: Review   pp 8,9

1 (1) before it got too warm
 (2) while I stirred the soup
 (3) if your mother agrees
 (4) where the supplies are stored

2 (1) where the yearbooks are kept
 (2) if he has a good excuse for being late
 (3) while you transport it
 (4) before the reporter began the news
 (5) before she started the washing machine

3 (1) after he ate some grass
 (2) because her characters were lifelike
 (3) when my bike had a flat tire
 (4) that the judges gave her top scores

4 (1) because we don't know a word's meaning
 (2) after she poured the cake batter into the pan
 (3) that he memorized it
 (4) when it was their turn to perform
 (5) because she wants to improve

5 **Complex Sentences: Review** pp 10,11

1 (1) Since our team improved, we
  (2) Since the planetarium closed, they
  (3) Since Peter had swimming lessons, he
  (4) Since summer began, more
  (5) Since the motorcycle broke down, its

2 (1) If the company advertises, more
  (2) If the jacket is reversible, you
  (3) If we take a different route, we
  (4) If she wants to learn more, she
  (5) If we leave our cat home alone, she

3 (1) Although he doesn't speak English, he
  (2) Although reptiles and birds are different, they
  (3) Although the painting was not complete, it
  (4) Although the tribes didn't have coins or dollars, they

4 (1) As I had to meet a friend, I
  (2) As my brother didn't save his allowance, he
  (3) As we all play instruments, we
  (4) As the current was strong, they
  (5) As apples are nutritious, we

6 **Independent and Dependent Clauses** pp 12,13

1 (1) Tornadoes can occur in spring
  (2) The nature reserve is large
  (3) The puppy limped
  (4) You need glasses

2 (1) The star player shot the ball.
  (2) The sea rose substantially.
  (3) We raised money.
  (4) The teacher said, "Time is up."

3 (1) The leaves have changed color
  (2) Elephants roam
  (3) the man wore a heavy suit
  (4) I am grateful
  (5) She brought her blanket

4 (1) A fossil was found
  (2) The bird could fly
  (3) I like to ride my bike
  (4) Bill loved to sing along
  (5) He sold a comic book

7 **Independent and Dependent Clauses** pp 14,15

1 (1) If there is an emergency,
  (2) until we couldn't anymore.
  (3) before we could catch it.
  (4) If it begins to rain,
  (5) where he could see all the players.

2 (1) DC (2) IC (3) DC (4) DC (5) IC

3 (1) <u>Although he has read many types of books,</u> (he likes historical fiction the best.)
  (2) (Radio stations broadcast popular songs) <u>until people no longer like them.</u>
  (3) <u>Before I go to bed,</u> (I always brush my teeth.)
  (4) (The inventor believed in his device) <u>before anyone else liked it.</u>
  (5) <u>After she writes a story,</u> (she draws corresponding illustrations.)

4 (1) where they could hike to an old fort
  (2) since we celebrated Thanksgiving
  (3) before we could finish our game
  (4) Until Mom wakes up,
  (5) Although he loves strawberry ice cream,

8 **Independent and Dependent Clauses** pp 16,17

1 (1) Maya hopes to exhibit her photographs
  (2) we go to the pool
  (3) they have been playing outside longer
  (4) Protesters marched
  (5) my sister persisted

2 (1) After I took a nap
  (2) even though the oven door was closed
  (3) so every passing person would see
  (4) Before the show ended
  (5) while my brother captured the flag

3 [SAMPLE ANSWERS]
(1) the girl washed the dishes / the girl washed the plates
(2) she read a mystery / she read a thriller
(3) we can catch the movie / we can catch the movie trailers
(4) A whale surfaced / The creature surfaced
(5) My dad carried the bag / My father carried the bag
(6) The kids rode skateboards / Some kids rode skateboards
(7) The girl wants to be an astronaut / The girl wants to go to outer space
(8) The boy lifted his trophy / The boy lifted his award
(9) The little bunnies hopped / The rabbits hopped
(10) They practiced karate / The people practiced karate

9 Noun Clauses

pp 18, 19

1 (1) why leaves change color
(2) that she didn't ace her test
(3) how he performed the trick
(4) where the bandleader walked
(5) how the play would end

2 (1) that she could wear her favorite dress
(2) how the coach did the jump
(3) that we finished our essays on time
(4) what my friend was thinking

3 (1) when the movie takes place
(2) why glue is sticky
(3) what I want to be when I grow up
(4) how she got electricity from a potato
(5) where the post office was
(6) where the kitten went
(7) why the guinea pig was sick
(8) how he bakes the cake
(9) when the county fair would start
(10) where the forest fires began

10 Noun Clauses

pp 20, 21

1 (1) My mom was hoping
  That it would not rain during the football game.
(2) Carla liked to jog where there were no cars.
(3) Everyone agreed
  that we should get tickets for the fashion show.
(4) The man read
  where the fireworks would happen.
(5) Anybody could guess
  what the ending of the book might be.

2 (1) why (2) what (3) where (4) when (5) how

3 (1) why the moon eclipses the sun
(2) what the character does
(3) how he whistles
(4) where public transportation is located
(5) when we would pick pumpkins
(6) how people write computer programs
(7) what the government program is about
(8) how telescopes work
(9) why mosquito bites itch
(10) that comic books can be valuable

11 Noun Clauses

pp 22, 23

1 (1) why the children quarreled
(2) what you do with the herbs
(3) how athletes train for a competition
(4) where the bridge leads
(5) when the vegetables will be ready to harvest

2 (1) when everyone had arrived
(2) that she was elected class secretary
(3) how the memorial will look
(4) how a cavity forms
(5) where he could drop us off

3 (1) why a porcupine raises its quills
[SAMPLE ANSWERS]
(2) when the soccer match was on TV / when his favorite team is playing soccer
(3) how chemicals react with one another / how the experiment works
(4) where my favorite book is located / where the librarian sits
(5) what their older siblings were doing / what the older kids were playing
(6) how the sailboat moves across the water using wind / how the sailboat floats
(7) what it might be like if aliens invaded / what aliens might be like
(8) where there are no trees / where the ground is level
(9) why dinosaurs went extinct / why dinosaurs no longer roamed the earth
(10) when we planned on moving / when we would see each other again

12 Adverb Clauses
pp 24, 25

1 (1) before she went to preschool
(2) until he became a millionaire
(3) if my mother would read it
(4) because her parents spoke different languages
(5) until his parents got home

2 (1) until he moved
(2) when they start to pile up
(3) because he received a diploma
(4) after our cat became ill

3 (1) When our teacher returned,
(2) Because her dog loved her,
(3) Although the show wasn't popular,
(4) If the hydrant is opened,
(5) After the chauffeur dropped her off,
(6) because she was thirsty
(7) Although the flutist was nervous,
(8) If a bungalow is available,
(9) until he liked his outfit
(10) because they finished first

13 Adverb Clauses
pp 26, 27

1 (1) <u>I didn't enjoy tennis lessons</u> until I learned to serve.
(2) <u>The scientist did an experiment</u> because he wanted to find a cure.
(3) <u>We could save more trees</u> if people used paper more carefully.
(4) <u>I think of Martin Luther King, Jr.</u> when I think of activism.
(5) Although the horses were strong, <u>they pulled the sleigh slowly.</u>

2 (1) until (2) If (3) whenever (4) after (5) Before

3 (1) because he had eaten too much
(2) when she measured angles
(3) Although you may disagree
(4) before he traveled outside of the country
(5) when we had a snow day
(6) After I saw a documentary about Amelia Earhart
(7) whenever it is Thanksgiving
(8) because they wanted more space
(9) because they create clean energy
(10) Before she made friends

14 Adverb Clauses
pp 28, 29

1 (1) when I stopped by the gymnasium
(2) because fiction stories are not real
(3) if the columnist writes about the baseball team
(4) even though that commercial showed Lake Tahoe
(5) after she bowled a perfect game

2 (1) after we decorated for Halloween
(2) if he eats nuts
(3) because it wanted to reduce traffic
(4) before explorers arrived
(5) although he shaved that morning

3 [SAMPLE ANSWERS]
(1) although it was raining / although we got wet
(2) before I caught the bus / before I left the house
(3) if we washed the dishes / if we cleaned up dinner
(4) because she studied each night / because she worked very hard
(5) though the weather report said it would rain / though the newspaper said it might rain
(6) because flash floods were common / because flooding was possible
(7) before he dunked it / before he scored
(8) because it was easy to dance to / because it was so catchy
(9) while I brought out the hockey sticks / while I got the equipment
(10) after our dog ran away / after our dog got lost

15 Adjective Clauses

pp 30, 31

1 (1) where my father works
(2) that we will donate
(3) who chaperoned the field trip
(4) that I will enter into a contest
(5) that we look forward to

2 (1) that was difficult to win
(2) who are respectful
(3) that had chickens and goats
(4) that has a large screen

3 (1) that recognized academic achievement
(2) who was an asthma expert
(3) where the soccer team practices
(4) that was inhabited by wild horses
(5) that promoted pet adoption
(6) that my grandmother gave to me
(7) who practice regularly
(8) that are good for baking
(9) that Mrs. Alvarez advises
(10) that was mainly rocks and dirt

16 Adjective Clauses

pp 32, 33

1 (1) The school had a program that encouraged healthy eating.
(2) I ran a 5 kilometer race, which is not long compared to a half marathon.
(3) The costume that I wore last year is too small to fit me now.
(4) We made a haystack, which later fell.

2 (1) where (2) that (3) that (4) that (5) which

3 (1) that required dice
(2) where I take violin lessons
(3) which she made from sheets
(4) where authors were signing books
(5) that attracted robins and sparrows
(6) that wasted a lot of water
(7) which inspired the students
(8) who was an excellent athlete
(9) who was a talented face painter
(10) where you will see many colors and shapes

17 Adjective Clauses

pp 34, 35

1 (1) who (2) that (3) who (4) that (5) who

2 (1) who (2) that (3) who (4) who (5) that

3 [SAMPLE ANSWERS]
(1) that always gets into trouble / that likes to chew shoes
(2) which were different sizes / which were different
(3) where bicycles were fixed / where bikes were repaired
(4) who like to sing / who like music
(5) that had an exhibit on King Tut / that displayed mummies
(6) which had a toy inside / which made him happy
(7) who entered through the window / who tried to steal many things
(8) that is held annually / that our town organizes
(9) who just won the race / who just crossed the finish line
(10) that has lots of scary monsters in it / that has scary stories in it

© Kumon Publishing Co., Ltd.

18 Review: Clauses
pp 36, 37

1 (1) what (2) when (3) why
(4) how (5) where

2 (1) after (2) if (3) whenever
(4) until (5) before

3 (1) that (2) where (3) who
(4) who (5) which

4 (1) The cat sleeps (whenever she can.) / adverb clause

(2) I wondered
(how a cactus can live for so long without water.) /
noun clause

(3) I will take a bus (if the subway isn't running.) / adverb
clause

(4) The vase (that he broke) was inexpensive. / adjective
clause

(5) She asked (what the book was about.) / noun clause

19 Three-Paragraph Essay: Review
pp 38, 39

1 (1) best friends
(2) ancient Greece
(3) plan a luau party
(4) England
(5) good night's rest

2 Underneath New York City's spectacular skyscrapers
is the equally impressive subway system.

3 (1) Panda cubs are extremely fragile infants.
(2) Coral reefs are important and must be protected.

20 Three-Paragraph Essay: Review
pp 40, 41

1 (1) Many people believe that the one-dollar bill should
be part of the United States' past.
(2) the government $5.6 billion
(3) Paper money
(4) countries
(5) metal sheets / public transportation agencies

2 (1) Every March, the United States celebrates Women's
History Month, but it wasn't always that way.
(2) How did this change come about?
(3) Sadly, it wasn't until the 1970s that women
in the United States would lobby for such a
commemoration.
(4) While Women's History Week was a victory, it was
just the beginning.
(5) That historical change is affecting schools and
communities today.

21 Three-Paragraph Essay: Review
pp 42, 43

1 (1) If I could plan a town, I would allow only public
transportation and bicycles.
(2) Though this plan is extreme, there are many
benefits to this idea.
(3) The roads would have less traffic, and people could
commute easily.
(4) Lastly, biking, which is a great form of exercise,
would be encouraged.
(5) In closing, if I could plan a town, I would organize it
around public transportation and bicycles.

2 (1) Animals should be used in films, but only with strict
regulation.
(2) In the 1940s, cruel and hazardous practices used
with animal actors were prohibited.
(3) not all animals can enjoy a good life outside the
wild.
(4) They perform important roles, can educate the
public, and are adored by audiences.
(5) The debate over using animals in movies is
complicated,

22 Three-Paragraph Essay: Review
pp 44, 45

1 (1) Nature can be incredibly powerful and perform
many destructive and dazzling feats.
(2) Keep an eye out during a thunderstorm for "ball
lightning."
(3) One Serbian town even experienced a frog shower
one day!
(4) If it is pushed by strong winds, this snow can roll
into logs, which are called "snow rollers."
(5) In conclusion, nature has a lot of astonishing
powers that can create strange, damaging, and
exciting events.

2 [SAMPLE ANSWERS]

Main Idea:

friendly, make the neighborhood safer, and act in everyone's best interest.

Supporting Details 1:

- Good neighbors say hello and are polite.
- Small gestures like waving or asking how a person's day is going make the neighborhood feel warm and welcoming.
- Some neighbors even host parties for the neighborhood.

Supporting Details 2:

- Good neighbors make sure everyone is safe.
- They may do that by keeping their dogs on leashes or by training their dogs to be friendly.
- They also drive slowly and carefully in the neighborhood.

Supporting Details 3:

- Good neighbors take good care of their homes so that the neighborhood is a nice place to live.
- They put garbage in the proper place.
- They also recycle.

Conclusion:

being a good neighbor takes effort but makes the neighborhood a great place to live. Being polite and friendly, keeping the neighborhood safe, and being a good citizen are all ways to make a neighborhood a great place to live.

23 Five-Paragraph Essay — pp 46,47

1 (1) A　(2) D　(3) B　(4) C　(5) B

24 Five-Paragraph Essay: Choosing a Topic — pp 48,49

1 [SAMPLE ANSWERS]

(1) movie / book
(2) visit many different countries / give speeches at schools
(3) heights / the dark
(4) clean up a park / tutor younger children
(5) Canada / Japan

2 (1) ANSWERS MAY VARY
(2) ANSWERS MAY VARY
(3) ANSWERS MAY VARY

25 Five-Paragraph Essay: Topic Sentences — pp 50,51

1 (1) Essay's main idea: Woodpeckers can knock their bills into trees repeatedly.
Supporting paragraphs' main ideas:
① dense skulls
② small brains
③ little fluid in their heads

(2) Essay's main idea: Regular exercise has many health benefits besides fitness.
Supporting paragraphs' main ideas:
① boosts memory
② improves mood
③ reduces stress

(3) Essay's main idea: The school play takes a lot of work and preparation.
Supporting paragraphs' main ideas:
① build the set
② rehearse and memorize lines
③ promote opening night

2 (1) Topic: My best friend
Essay's main idea: My best friend is generous.
Supporting paragraph's main idea:
She shares her treat with me.

(2) Topic: Studying
Essay's main idea: The best ways to study
Supporting paragraph's main idea:
Read the notes you took in class.

(3) Topic: Sports
Essay's main idea: Good sportsmanship
Supporting paragraph's main idea: Play fairly

(4) Topic: Recycling
Essay's main idea: Reasons to recycle
Supporting paragraph's main idea:
To save precious resources

(5) Topic: If you are lost
Essay's main idea: How to get help
Supporting paragraph's main idea:
Find a police officer to assist you

26 Five-Paragraph Essay: Introductory Paragraph — pp 52,53

1 [SAMPLE ANSWERS]

(1) There are many reasons why wolves should be protected in Wyoming. There are few of them left, and they improve their ecosystem's well-being. Their actions also help other animals.

(2) Referees play an important role in sports, as they ensure fair play, settle disputes, and keep games moving quickly.

2 [SAMPLE ANSWERS]
(1) Droughts greatly affect the environment by ruining food crops, increasing the risk of wildfires, and limiting drinking water. While most weather patterns last for a short time, droughts can last for many years. Such long periods without water can have devastating effects on anything that needs water to live and grow.
(2) You can lead an earthquake drill by making a plan in case of an earthquake, teaching your class or group what to do, and practicing. Although earthquakes typically occur in certain areas, they can happen anywhere and at any time. Leading an earthquake drill isn't difficult, and the first step is making a smart plan.

27 **Five-Paragraph Essay: Supporting Paragraphs** pp 54,55

1 (1) Governments should spend more money to explore space because this exploration gets people interested in the sciences.
(2) Furthermore, more space exploration leads to innovation in science and technology, which is an essential part of a strong economy.
(3) Besides spurring the economy with innovation, space exploration creates jobs.

2 (1) His work is read in at least eighty languages, including Chinese, Armenian, Bengali, and many more.
(2) He coined more than one thousand words, many of which are still frequently used.
(3) For example, in *A Midsummer Night's Dream,* four separate plots interact and end with a happy marriage.

28 **Five-Paragraph Essay: Supporting Details** pp 56,57

1 (1) ⓐ (2) ⓒ (3) ⓑ

2 (1) ANSWERS MAY VARY
(2) ANSWERS MAY VARY

3 ANSWERS MAY VARY

Hint: A supporting paragraph should include a topic sentence and sentences with supporting details, facts, and / or examples.

29 **Five-Paragraph Essay: Transition Sentences** pp 58,59

1 (1) ⓐ (2) ⓒ (3) ⓒ

2 (1) As a result of such recent discoveries, some wonder what else is unknown.
(2) ANSWERS MAY VARY
(3) ANSWERS MAY VARY
(4) ANSWERS MAY VARY
(5) ANSWERS MAY VARY

Hint: A transition sentence should help the reader anticipate the next paragraph.

30 **Five-Paragraph Essay: Conclusion** pp 60,61

1 (1) Carbon monoxide poisoning is preventable.
(2) Have all your gas-, oil-, and coal-burning appliances checked by a technician every year.
(3) Install a battery-operated carbon monoxide detector in your home, and check the batteries often.
(4) Seek medical help if you feel dizzy, light-headed, or nauseous.
(5) In conclusion, these three steps can help you prevent carbon monoxide poisoning.

2 (1) ANSWERS MAY VARY
(2) ANSWERS MAY VARY

31 **Five-Paragraph Essay: Outlining** pp 62,63

1 (1) Main idea of supporting paragraph 3
(2) Topic sentence of supporting paragraph 1
(3) Supporting detail
(4) Restatement of introduction's topic sentence
(5) Concluding sentence

2 (1) Peer pressure is harmful if kids' peers make unhealthy choices.
(2) Wearing certain clothes to try to fit in can harm self-esteem.
(3) Nevertheless, kids should recognize how their peer group influences them.
(4) Peer pressure can be good or bad, and kids should be mindful of its impact.
(5) Peers can prompt positive actions, too.

1 (1) snowboarding / beautiful / dedicated / January / people / indoors
(2) ⓐ Skiing and snowboarding are great winter sports because you can spend time outside, see beautiful landscapes, and keep healthy during the winter months.
ⓑ There is even a month dedicated to skiing and snowboarding—January is Learn to Ski and Snowboard Month.
(3) January may be a time when most people stay indoors, but it is a wonderful month to head into the great outdoors.
(4) ⓓ / ⓔ / ⓕ / ⓖ / ⓗ

33 **Five-Paragraph Essay** pp 66,67

1 ANSWERS MAY VARY

Hint: Choose a topic that inspires many ideas. A good topic to write about will have three main ideas and some supporting details.

2 ANSWERS MAY VARY

Hint: Use your outline as a detailed plan for your essay. Refer back to your outline as you complete each section, or as often as necessary.

34 **Review** pp 68,69

1 (1) , "You have ten more minutes of recess."
(2) , "I'll race you to the water fountain."
(3) , "You're on!"
(4) , "Did you study for the science test?"
(5) , "Of course!"

2 (1) that the plane will depart on time
(2) that she is afraid of flying
(3) that flying is very safe
(4) that he is excited for their trip
(5) that they look at their itinerary

3 (1) We drank cider
after we picked apples. / adverb clause
(2) This treasure map showed
where the pirates had to go. / noun clause
(3) We went to swim practice
before we did our homework. / adverb clause
(4) I asked the expert who knew a lot about it. / adjective clause
(5) We bought tickets, which were for the wrong date. / adjective clause
(6) I go hiking whenever the weather is good. / adverb clause
(7) The boy wondered
what walking on the moon is like. / noun clause
(8) The teacher will give a quiz
if we finish this chapter today. / adverb clause
(9) This is the classroom
where we do science experiments. / adjective clause
(10) He asked what my essay was about. / noun clause

35 **Review** pp 70,71

1 ANSWERS MAY VARY

Hint: You can also use an outline to brainstorm ideas for your essay.

2 ANSWERS MAY VARY

Hint: Your five-paragraph essay should include an introduction, three supporting paragraphs, and a conclusion.